Dining Out in Hungary

Angéla F. Nagy

Dining Out in Hungary

Corvina

Translated by Judith Elliott
Series designed by Julianna Rácz
Cover photo by Péter Korniss
taken in one of the dining rooms
of the Gundel Restaurant

Printed in Hungary

ISBN 963 13 3891 6

Preface

Dear Visitor,

I am sure you are familiar with some of our Hungarian dishes, indeed perhaps it was our culinary art which enticed you to come. When you open the menu in a good Hungarian restaurant, you will find, that contrary to common belief that we eat nothing but goulash and stew, there are numerous different dishes to choose from, many with names shrouded in mystery.

The purpose of this book is to make your choice easier. Among the many traditional dishes, there are some that earned their names from the chefs who created them and others that are linked to famous individuals in Hungarian history or to different regions of the country.

On your return home you can relive your memories of Hungarian cuisine by preparing some of the dishes you most enjoyed.

These recipes are for four portions with the exception of the desserts.

Contents

A note on terminology: since the names of certain foods are not identical in American and British English, we provide a brief glossary of frequently used terms below.

American	British
bacon slices	bacon rashers
baking pan	baking tin
bouillon	broth
broil, broiled	grill, grilled
can, canned	tin, tinned
candy, candies	sweets, confectionery
cook book	cookery book
cottage cheese	curd cheese
glazed fruit	glacé fruit
powdered sugar	icing sugar
process	liquify
seedless raisins	sultanas
sour cream	soured cream
squash	vegetable marrow
unmold	turn out
whipping cream	double cream

Soups

Újházy chicken soup

Pethes soup

Soup with liver dumplings

Palóc soup

Jókai bean soup

Fiancé soup

Gulyás soup

Szeged fish soup

Fish soup for hangovers

Fruit soup

Újházy Chicken Soup

Újházy tyúkhúsleves

Ede Újházy was one of the most famous actors
at the turn of the century. He won tremendous
acclaim for his rendition of Shylock at the Pest
National Theatre. The audiences adored him. His
vivacious spirits and healthy appetite made him
a lively and much sought after guest among
restauranteurs. However, he followed
a bohemian life style and was often short of
money, though this did not stop him from sitting
at his usual table in the then well known
Gambrinus Restaurant and modestly ordering
a soup. It was on such an occasion that the chef
decided to give Újházy a surprise and serve him
a soup that he would never forget. The bowl
placed before him was a meal in itself, for it
contained meat, vegetables and pasta to make
it even more satisfying. It was not long before
other guests at the restaurant became curious
about this special soup and ordered it for
themselves. Soon the whole of Budapest had
heard of the soup and hence, under the name of
Újházy Chicken Soup, it took its place among
the traditional dishes of Hungarian cuisine.

INGREDIENTS
**500 g (1 lb 2 oz) lean flank of beef * 1–1^1/$_2$ kg (2–2^1/$_2$lb)
chicken * 200 g (7 oz) beef bones * 4 carrots *
3 parsnips * 100 g (4 oz) kohlrabi * 100 g (4 oz) celeriac
*250 g (9 oz) peas (fresh or frozen) * 150 g (5 oz) green
beans * 1 tomato * 1 yellow or green pepper * 150 g
(5 oz) mushrooms * 1 large onion * 100 g (4 oz) savoy
cabbage * 10 peppercorns * ^{1}/$_2$ tsp caraway seed * ^{1}/$_4$ tsp
dried bay leaf * turmeric * 3 cloves * pinch nutmeg
*handful of thin small pasta**

Prepare the vegetables. Cut the beef and chicken into four pieces. Place the beef and the beef bones into a large pan, pour in enough cold water to cover, add the spices (peppercorns, bay leaf, caraway seeds, cloves, nutmeg and turmeric), and simmer until the meat is half cooked. Then add the carrots, parsnips, kohlrabi, celeriac, onion, tomato and pepper all left whole. Finally add the chicken pieces and pour in enough boiling water to cover well. Season with salt and simmer gently for 30 minutes. Slice the green beans and add the beans and peas to the pan. Continue to simmer until everything is tender. Then strain the soup into a pan and cook the pasta. While the pasta is cooking, remove the skin and bones from the chicken, cut into strips then return to the pan. Slice the carrot and parsnip and return to pan. Bring the soup to the boil and finally add the halved or quartered mushrooms. Simmer for a further 4 or 5 minutes, then serve.

Pethes Soup
Pethes leves

Imre Pethes was similar to Újházy in many ways. He lived in the same period and also gained success as an actor at the turn of the century, particular in the plays of Ibsen and Shakespeare. Like Újházy, he loved good food and after a theater production he would sit in the famous New York Coffee House for supper. The New York was not simply a coffee house, but a meeting place for writers, poets and artists. Life never stopped from morning till night beneath the glittering chandeliers and bronze decorations. It was here that well known writers, budding poets and other literary figures gathered to discuss Hungarian culture. Masterpieces were created at the small marble tables. Pens and paper were automatically given when coffee was served. Painters, sculptors and actors frequented the coffee house and could order hot or cold food at any time of the day or night, and often on credit. The chief chef created excellent dishes in their honour and knowing Imre Pethes's passion for bone marrow, he created Pethes Soup.

INGREDIENTS

1000g (2¹/₄ lb) stewing beef * 1 large marrow bone *
4 carrots * 3 parsnips * 1 kohlrabi * 1 Savoy cabbage *
1 large onion * 1 tomató * 1 green or yellow pepper *
¹/₄ celeriac * salt * 3–4 peppercorns * ¹/₂tsp caraway
seeds * ¹/₂ tsp nutmeg * 1 bay leaf *1 bunch chives.
For the pasta: 1 egg * 100g (4 oz) plain flour * pinch salt

Leave the meat in one piece, place in a large pan and cover with water. Add the peppercorns, caraway seeds, nutmeg and bay leaf. Cover and simmer gently for 1 hour, removing the scum from time to time. Prepare the vegetables, leaving the carrots and parsnips whole and add to the soup. Pour 1¹/₂ liters (2³/₄ pints) of boiling water and continue to simmer until the meat is almost tender. Tie the marrow bone in cheese cloth or a thin kitchen towel and add to the pan. Cook for a further 20 minutes then remove from the pan.

While the soup is cooking prepare the pasta: sift the flour into a bowl adding a pinch of salt. Make a well in the center and gradually beat in the egg. Mix thoroughly, form into a ball and put aside for 30 minutes. Then roll out very thin and cut into narrow strips.

Strain the soup into a pan, add the pasta and cook until done. Add the sliced carrot and parsnip, the kohlrabi and celeriac. Cut the meat into 8 pieces, place into four soup bowls and put a piece of bone marrow on top. Spoon the soup over the meat and serve.

Soup with Liver Dumplings
Májgaluska leves

INGREDIENTS

500 g (1 lb 2 oz) beef bones * 3 carrots * 2 parsnips * 1 piece of kohlrabi * 1 piece celeriac * 1 medium onion * 1 clove garlic, left whole * 1 tomato * 1 green or yellow pepper * 1 meat stock cube * 5 peppercorns * $^1/_2$ tsp caraway seed * 1 small bay leaf * 1 bunch parsley. *For the liver dumplings:* 150 g (5 oz) liver * 1 roll soaked in a little milk * 1 tbs grated onion * 1 tbs oil * 1 egg *breadcrumbs * salt * pinch ground pepper * 1 tsp marjoram

Wash all the vegetables, leaving them whole. Wash the bones and put them all into a large pan. Pour in $1^1/_2$ liter ($2^3/_4$ pints) of boiling water. Add the stock cube and simmer until the vegetables are cooked. While the soup is cooking, squeeze out the excess milk from the roll and divide into crumbs. Fry the grated onion in a pan in the oil, stir in the finely chopped liver. Remove from the heat, tip into a bowl and blend with the roll and the beaten egg. Season with salt, pepper and the marjoram. Sprinkle with a few breadcrumbs to make a fairly stiff mixture. Then put aside.

When the soup is ready, strain into another pan. Divide the dumpling mixture into very small balls. Bring the strained soup to the boil, add the dumplings and cook for a few minutes.

Before serving return the carrot and parsnip to the pan, cut into thin slices and add the finely chopped parsley.

Palóc Soup
Palócleves

In the second half of the 19th century the Archduke István Hotel in Pest was one of the most famous and most elegant hotels not only in Hungary but throughout Europe. Gourmets were attracted to the hotel because of its kitchen, which was managed by the famous Hungarian chef János Gundel. His menus boasted oysters and crab from the Adriatic, fresh salmon from the Rhine and sturgeon from the Danube.

One frequent visitor to the hotel was Kálmán Mikszáth, one of the best known novelists of his time, who based his stories on the lives of the Hungarians living in Palóc, a region in the far north of the country. In honour of this great writer, János Gundel created Palóc soup, which is still very popular.

INGREDIENTS
**500 g (1 lb 2 oz) lamb or lean stewing beef * 2 tbs oil *
1 onion * 2 garlic cloves * 300 g (11 oz) potatoes *
500 g (1 lb 2 oz) green beans * 1 tbs flour *
100 ml (4 oz) sour cream * salt * 1 tsp paprika * pinch
dried bay leaf * pinch caraway seed**

Peel and finely chop the onion. Heat 1 tbs oil in a large saucepan and sauté the onion until translucent. Cut the meat into cubes and add to the pan. Fry over a high heat for a few minutes. Then turn down the heat and add the paprika, 2 liters (3½ pints) of boiling water, the garlic (left whole) and the spices. Cover and simmer until the meat is half cooked. Add the sliced green beans and the potato, peeled and cubed. Continue to simmer until the meat is tender. Make a light roux with the remaining oil and the flour. Stir in a little cold water and add to the soup. Bring to the boil and stir until the soup thickens. Pour in the sour cream and serve.

Jókai Bean Soup
Jókai bableves

Mór Jókai was one of the great Hungarian romantic novelists of the last century. His wife, Róza Laborfalvy, was not only an excellent actress but a very talented cook as witnessed by many great contemporary figures in Hungarian literary and theatrical circles. Jókai's favorite dish was bean soup and by the end of the 1860s it had already appeared as "Jókai style bean soup with pigs' trotters" on the menu of a well known restaurant in the town of Tata, where he lived. It soon became popular throughout the country and is still served in the best restaurants today, though it is now prepared with knuckle of pork.

INGREDIENTS

250 g (9 oz) dried kidney beans (soaked overnight in cold water) * 1 smoked pork knuckle * 2 carrots * 2 parsnips * 1 piece kohlrabi * 1 piece celeriac * 1 onion * 2–3 garlic cloves * 200 ml (7 oz) sour cream * 1 heaped tbs flour * 3–4 peppercorns * good pinch dried bay leaf * a little vinegar. *For the soup dumplings:* 1 egg * flour

Wash the knuckle, put in a large pan and add enough cold water to cover. Bring to the boil, cover and simmer until tender (approx. 50 minutes). Drain the beans, put into another pan and pour in the strained soup. Then add the carrots and parsnips (left whole), the celeriac and kohlrabi, the onion, garlic and finally the pepper and bay leaf. Add enough additional boiling water to make $1^1/2$ liters ($2^3/4$ pints) altogether. Cover and simmer until the vegetables are tender. Remove the carrots and parsnips.

While the soup is cooking prepare the pasta, beat the egg in a bowl and add enough flour to make a fairly stiff pliable mixture. Cover and put aside. Then dip the thumb and middle finger in flour and break off small pieces. Drop into the soup and cook until the noodles rise to the surface. Cut the carrots and parsnips into cubes and return to the soup together with the deboned and sliced knuckle. Blend the sour cream in a bowl with the flour until smooth, then add to the soup, stirring until it thickens. Finally add a few drops of vinegar to give a slightly tangy flavor.

Fiancé Soup
Vőlegény leves

The Mátyás Pince has been a very popular restaurant in Budapest for decades. The lively Gipsy music and first class cuisine attracts foreigners from all over the world. In the 70's a German gentleman began to visit the restaurant regularly, drawn to Budapest because he had fallen in love with a Hungarian girl. He was not in the prime of youth and was afraid of losing her. In desperation he turned to the chef of his favorite restaurant and asked him if he could possibly create a special dish which would enhance his virility. The dish the cook created was a soup and he called it "Fiancé soup".

We don't actually know whether the German succeeded in winning the girl's heart as a result of eating the soup, but Fiancé soup did become very popular and has been featured ever since on the menus of many of the good restaurants in Hungary, not to mention the Mátyás Pince.

INGREDIENTS

150 g (9oz) beef (leg) * ¹/₂ chicken * 300 g (11 oz) vegetables for soup (carrots, parsnips, kohlrabi) * 200 g (7 oz) celeriac * 1 onion * 2 egg yolks * 4 quail eggs * 100 ml (4 oz) single cream * 1 tbs tomato purée * salt * 5 peppercorns * ¹/₂ tsp caraway seed * 2 pinches dried bay leaf * pinch ground nutmeg * 1 bunch parsley * a little lemon juice

Cut the beef into two or three pieces. Put in a large pan and pour in enough water to cover. Bring to the boil, cover and simmer until the meat is half cooked. Then add the chicken cut in half, the prepared vegetables and celeriac cut in half. Pour in enough boiling water to make 1¹/₂ liters (2³/₄ pints) altogether. Add the tomato purée, the peppercorns, caraway seed, bay leaf and nutmeg and continue to simmer until the meat is tender. Strain the soup. Beat the cream and egg yolks in a bowl, then gradually add to the soup stirring constantly. Add a few drops of lemon juice, debone the chicken and cut into small cubes, cut the vegetables into cubes and return to the soup. Heat through but do not boil. Hard boil the quail eggs and place one in each soup bowl. Finally add the finely chopped parsley to the soup and spoon over the eggs.

Gulyás Soup

Gulyásleves (Bográcsgulyás)

The only thing we know about the origins of
this soup is that it was cooked in a cauldron
over an open fire. It was one of the soups
prepared by the cowherds *(gulyás)* who rode on
horseback and took their cattle to the fields to
graze. They would live there in small huts from
early spring until autumn. Their diet consisted
mainly of nutritious and filling soups.

Gulyás is now one of the most common meat
soups prepared in Hungarian homes and
restaurants.

INGREDIENTS

400 g (14 oz) lean stewing beef * 2 tbs oil * 3 carrots *
2 parsnips * 1 piece kohlrabi * 1 piece celeriac *
400 g (14 oz) potatoes * 1 onion * 2 garlic cloves * salt *
1 tbs paprika * 4 peppercorns * $^1/_2$ tsp caraway seed *
$^1/_2$ tsp dried bay leaf. Pasta for the soup (see Jókai bean
soup p. 15)

Sauté the peeled and finely chopped onion in the
oil in a large pan. Cut the meat into small cubes
and add to the pan. Fry over a high heat for a
few minutes. Then add the paprika and chopped
garlic. Add enough boiling water to cover, and
simmer with a lid on until the meat is half
cooked. Then add the prepared carrots, parsnips,
kohlrabi and celeriac cut into cubes, the
peppercorns, caraway seed and bay leaf. Season
with salt. Pour in enough boiling water to make
$1^1/_2$ liters ($2^3/_4$ pints) altogether. Bring to the boil
and cook for ten minutes. Then add the diced
potatoes and simmer until the meat and
vegetables are cooked. Finally drop in the

prepared noodles. When they rise to the surface simmer for another two to three minutes, then serve.

Szeged Fish Soup
Szegedi halászlé

In the middle of the last century Wilhelm Richter, a German traveler, came to Hungary and wrote down his most interesting experiences, which were later published in a guide book. He wrote that his visit to the River Tisza was one of the highlights, particularly the fish soup that some fishermen invited him to try. He described the supper cooked on the river bank in great detail: "....it was dusk when the men stopped fishing and made a huge fire. They hung a large cauldron over the crackling fire and melted a lot of fat. A handful of flour was then stirred in. Onion and salt and their lovely paprika was added and then the fish pieces. They told me that the stronger and redder the paprika and the larger the quantity of onion, the better the fish soup."

The preparation of fish soup has hardly changed in the last 150 years, though there are regional variations. The flavor of Tisza fish soup for example is quite different from that made around lake Balaton or by the Danube. Of all the Hungarian fish soups, however, the one prepared in the town of Szeged by the Tisza is still the best known. Obviously it is no longer cooked over an open fire, but you will still find it on the menus of numerous restaurants.

8 filets of carp or catfish * 500 g (1 lb 2 oz) small fish
(small white fish, small catfish, bream or tail and head of
carp) * 2 large onions * 1 level tbs fat or oil * salt *
1 tbs paprika * 1 tomato * 1 green or yellow pepper

Sauté the finely chopped onion in a large pan in
the fat until translucent. Wash and prepare the
small fish or head and tail of the carp and add to
the pan, along with the tomato and pepper. Pour
in enough water to cover. Bring to the boil, then
stir in the paprika and salt. Cover and simmer
for one hour. Then remove the fish bones and
strain through a sieve or process in an electric
blender. Strain into a large pan and add enough
water to make 1 1/2 liters (2 3/4 pints) altogether.
Bring to the boil then add the fish filets. Cover
and simmer for ten minutes. Serve piping hot
with slices of freshly baked bread.

Fish Soup for Hangovers
Korhely halászlé

In addition to its Fiancé soup, the Mátyás Pince
in Budapest is also famous for its fish dishes. It
is said that on one occasion a group went to
have lunch there after a particularly wild night.
Realizing their tender balance, the chef on duty
at the time offered to prepare a special fish soup
that would do wonders for their hangovers. This
is how this mild fish soup became accepted as a
remedy for an upset stomach and hangover. It is
often prepared in the early hours of the morning
after New Year's Eve parties.

INGREDIENTS
1 1/2 kg (3 3/4 lb) carp or 500 g (1 lb 2 oz) small catfish or
other small white fish with 500 g (1 lb 2 oz) carp filets *

2 onions * 200 ml (7 oz) sour cream * salt * freshly ground pepper * pinch paprika * 4 bay leaves * 2 slices lemon * lemon juice

---

Clean the fish carefully. If you are using only carp filet, put the backbone, head and tail into a large pan and cover with cold water. If you are using small fish, leave them whole. Bring to the boil, cover the pan and simmer for one hour, add the peeled and sliced onion and simmer for another 30 minutes. Then strain through a sieve or put in a blender to remove the bones. Return to the pan, season with salt, a pinch of pepper and the bay leaf. Add enough water to make 1 1/2 liters (2 3/4 pints) altogether. Bring to the boil, sprinkle with the paprika and add the fileted carp. Simmer for 15 minutes. Sprinkle with a little lemon juice to give it a slightly tangy flavour, and add the slices of lemon. Cover and simmer for a further five minutes. Finally stir in the sour cream, heat and serve.

Fruit Soup

Gyümölcsleves

INGREDIENTS

500 g (1 lb 2 oz) fruit (cherries, sour cherries, strawberries, raspberries, red currants, apricots or plums, or a mixture) * 200 ml (7 oz) single cream * 200 ml (7 oz) full bodied red wine (optional) * 50–100 g (2–4 oz) powdered sugar * pinch salt * ground cinnamon

---

Wash the fruit, remove the pits if necessary, then cut into slices, putting a few aside for decoration. Liquify the rest, add sugar to taste, the cream and 200 ml (7 oz) cold water (if you are using red fruits substitute the water for the wine). Blend thoroughly and pour into a bowl.

Pour in enough cold water to make 1 liter ($1^3/_4$ pints). Add a pinch of salt and chill. A pinch of ground nutmeg can be added to morello or plum soup. Serve straight from the refrigerator, poured into separate bowls. Decorate with the fruit. (Fruit soup is sometimes served hot, but it is better cold.)

Starters

Jellied pork

Hungarian foie gras

Hortobágy stuffed pancakes

Jellied Pork
Kocsonya

According to popular belief, it is thanks to two young boys that this delicious cold dish was discovered. Apparently in the middle of winter when every family in the village kills a pig, an economically minded woman made a soup from the ears and tail that others would throw away. She put the pan in the cold larder. Later on the young children of the house, so the story goes, began to feel rather peckish and hunted around to see what they could find. They went to the larder and helped themselves to some of the then jellied soup. Their mother, instead of punishing them, became curious and tried some herself. She liked it so much she decided to serve it to the family and guests as a cold starter. It was such a success that it was often seen on her table. It is now very popular and is offered in restaurants and in the home alike. *Kocsonya* has to be prepared the day before serving.

INGREDIENTS

2 pig's trotters * 1 pig's tail * 1 lean pork knuckle with the skin attached * 400 g (14 oz) lean leg, hand or shoulder of pork * 2 carrots * 1 parsnip * 2 onions * 3 garlic cloves * salt * 5 peppercorns

Clean the meat, carrots and parsnips. Cut the leg of pork into large cubes. Leave the carrots, parsnips, onion and garlic whole. Place in a large pan with the trotters, tail and knuckle and pour in enough cold water to cover. Season with salt and the peppercorns. Bring to the boil, then cover and simmer very gently until the meat falls off the bone. Leave overnight in a cold place, but do not refrigerate. The following day, carefully scrape off the fat. Heat until the aspic becomes liquid, lift out the meat and debone. Cut into cubes. Arrange the pieces of pork not too close together in a shallow, wide serving bowl or individual soup dishes. Then strain the liquid over the meat through a sieve and 2 layers of cheesecloth or thin cotton. Leave to set in a cold place. After it is set, it can be stored uncovered in the refrigerator. Serve with pickled horseradish or potato salad with slices of onion marinated in a mixture of vinegar and water and seasoned with salt and sugar.

Jellied pork can be made more attractive by serving it in a large fluted mould. Follow the recipe above, then pour a little of the strained stock into the bottom of the mould. Leave to set, then arrange the meat on top and pour over the rest of the stock. Leave to set before turning out onto a serving plate. Wrap the mould in a hot cloth or bathe briefly in hot water to ease unmoulding. Decorate with slices of hard boiled egg and gherkin. Cut into wedges and serve immediately.

Hungarian Foie Gras
Libamáj zsírjában

The liver of force-fed geese is a real Hungarian speciality. Goose liver is often served fried in slices and served flambee with brandy, or breaded and deep fried or added to letcho (Hungarian ratatouille, see p. 42), but the queen of goose liver dishes is foie gras cooked in goose fat. Every cook swears that their version is the best. We think ours is.

700–800 g (1³/₄ lb) goose liver * **1000g (2¹/₂ lb) goose fat** *
3 garlic cloves * **meat stock** * **pinch paprika**

Place half the goose fat in the bottom of a thick
bottomed pan. Lay the washed liver on top of
the fat, then cover with the remaining fat. Strain
enough meat stock to cover. Cook for 10
minutes per 100 g (4 oz) liver. To test if it is
cooked, prick with a meat skewer; if no pink
liquid escapes, the liver is done. Lift out the
liver with a perforated spoon and place in a
fireproof dish. Cook the stock and fat until all
the liquid has evaporated. Remove from heat,
stir in the paprika and strain through a fine
sieve. Pour over the hot liver. When cool store
in the refrigerator until the fat hardens. Serve
with freshly baked bread, thin slices of onion or
leeks. Spread the bread with the goose fat.

Hortobágy Stuffed Pancakes
Hortobágyi palacsinta

Károly Gundel, the chef of the famous Gundel
Restaurant in Budapest, created this delicious
starter and named it after the great Hungarian
plains. It may also be eaten as a main course.

INGREDIENTS
12 savoury pancakes (see p. 70) * **2 cooked chicken breasts
(it is best to use the breasts from the Chicken Paprika, see
p. 60)**

Remove the chicken breasts from the cooked
paprika chicken and dice or mince. Mix with
a little of the creamy paprika sauce from the

paprika chicken. Stuff the pancakes and roll
them up. Cover with a little more sauce and heat
through in the oven or microwave. (Left over
paprika veal or pork can also be used instead of
chicken.)

Salads

Csekonics salad

Lettuce salad

Cucumber salad

Mixed pickled salad

Csekonics Salad
Csekonics saláta

"I'm not a Csekonics" is a Hungarian saying used when someone asks for something beyond the other person's means–financial or otherwise. Gyula Csekonics was the black sheep of an ancient aristocratic family. His father, grandfather and great grandfather all became famous horse breeders, were prominent figures in political life and offered a lot of charity for the poor. By the middle of the last century, however, the youngest Csekonics had become notorious for his riotous and scandalous behaviour.

He was a compulsive gambler who never missed a horse race. He squandered huge sums of money. The whole of Pest and Buda buzzed with gossip about the latest escapades of Gyula Csekonics. The chef of Wampetics Inn, where the Gundel Restaurant now stands, named this rich salad after him.

INGREDIENTS
400 g (14 oz) cooked chicken breast * 25 king prawns * 300 g (11 oz) firm tomatoes * 1 large lettuce * salt * $^{1}/_{2}$ tsp caraway seed * 1 bunch parsley.
For the mayonnaise: 2 egg yolks * 200 ml (7 oz) oil * 1 liqueur glass brandy * 100 ml (4 oz) single cream * salt * pinch sugar * pinch cayenne pepper * 1 tsp mustard * a few drops tarragon vinegar * a few fresh tarragon leaves * slices of lemon for garnish

Bone and skin the chicken and cut into thin strips. Leave a few prawns whole and chop the rest into a bowl. Sprinkle with a little salt and add the caraway seed and the chopped parsley. Slice the tomatoes then halve the slices and add

to the bowl. Wash and drain the lettuce, put a
few nice lettuce leaves aside (enough to line the
serving dish) and roughly chop the rest. For the
mayonnaise: beat the egg yolks in a bowl and
gradually beat in the oil, drop by drop. As the
mayonnaise thickens, the oil may be added in
a thin stream. Then beat in the mustard, salt to
taste, the sugar, cayenne pepper and a few drops
of vinegar and the chopped tarragon. Leave to
chill. Beat the cream and cognac together
thoroughly, then lightly stir in the chicken
pieces, the prawns and tomato. Chill in the
refrigerator for one hour before adding the
chopped lettuce. Line a serving bowl with the
whole lettuce leaves and spoon in the salad.
Garnish with the prawns and the slices of lemon.
Serve very chilled with the mayonnaise in a
separate bowl.

Lettuce Salad

Fejessaláta

INGREDIENTS
1 large or 2 small round heads of lettuce * 1 heaped tbs
powdered sugar * salt * vinegar

This is a traditional way of preparing lettuce
salad in Hungary. Make the dressing by
blending 1–2 tbs vinegar with the same amount
of water. Add the sugar and salt to taste and stir
until the sugar dissolves. Wash and chop the
lettuce into strips and toss in the dressing just
before serving.

Cucumber Salad
Uborkasaláta

INGREDIENTS

800 g (1³/₄ lb) cucumber * 3 garlic cloves * 1 level tbs
powdered sugar * 1 level tsp salt * pinch paprika *
pinch freshly ground pepper * vinegar

Wash the cucumber then cut into very thin
slices. Place in a bowl, toss in the salt and
crushed garlic, cover and chill in the refrigerator
for 2–3 hours. Then add the sugar and enough
vinegar to give a pleasantly piquant flavour.
Chill for another 30 minutes, then serve
sprinkled with a little paprika and pepper.

Mixed Pickled Salad
Csalamádé

Most restaurants prepare their own salad using
fresh vegetables.

INGREDIENTS

500 g (1 lb 2 oz) white cabbage * 500 g (1 lb 2 oz)
cucumber * 500 g (1 lb 2 oz) green or yellow pepper *
500 g (1 lb 2 oz) onion * 250 g (9 oz) carrots *
250 g (9 oz) parsnips * 250 g (9 oz) green tomatoes *freshly
ground pepper * 1 tsp mustard seed * oil *mixture of
vinegar and water (half quantity of vinegar to water)
seasoned to taste with powdered sugar and salt

Core the cabbage. Shred or slice very thinly the
cabbage, onion and cucumber into a bowl and
mix together. Cut the prepared carrots, parsnips,
green tomatoes and cored peppers into thin
slices and add to the bowl. Season with ground
pepper and the mustard seed. Put the vinegar

and water dressing into a pan and bring to the boil. Pour over the salad while still hot, cover and leave overnight. Then tightly pack the vegetables into a screw top jar. Pour in enough liquid to cover, and add a pinch of salicylic acid. Seal the jars tightly and store in a cool place. Before serving toss in a little oil.

Vegetables and Pasta

Creamy potatoes

Hungarian green beans

Hungarian vegetable marrow

Spinach Hungarian style

Kohlrabi, carrots or peas Hungarian style

Kidney beans, split peas or lentils Hungarian style

Dumplings (Galuska)

Egg barley (Tarhonya)

Hungarians like vegetables cooked in their own way. They are not simply boiled or steamed and served with a nob of butter, but made more substantial by adding a roux or sour cream mixed with flour. For four portions use 1 kg (2¹/₄ lb) of vegetables.

Creamy Potatoes
Burgonyafőzelék

INGREDIENTS
1 kg (2¹/₄ lb) potatoes * 2 tbs oil * 1 tbs grated onion * 200 ml (7 oz) sour cream * good pinch paprika * salt * 1–2 bay leaves * 1 tbs flour

---

Sauté the onions in the oil until translucent. Sprinkle in the paprika and stir in the peeled and sliced potatoes. Season with salt. Add the bay leaves and a little boiling water. Cover and simmer until tender, adding a little more boiling water to stop the potato from sticking. Blend the sour cream and flour until smooth, pour into the pan and stir until the liquid thickens.

Hungarian Style Green Beans
Zöldbabfőzelék

Use the same ingredients as for the potato dish, substituting 1 kg (1¹/₄ lb) green beans for the potatoes and using 1–2 crushed garlic cloves and 1 bunch chopped parsley or dill instead of the bay leaf.

Follow the recipe above, adding the green beans sliced into 2 cm (1 in) pieces to the pan, together with the crushed garlic, chopped parsley or dill. Salt to taste, add a little boiling water and simmer until tender, pouring in additional boiling water from time to time as the liquid evaporates. Thicken with the sour cream and flour as described above.

Hungarian Style Vegetable Marrow (Squash)
Tökfőzelék

Use same ingredients and method as for Hungarian creamy style potatoes, substituting 1 kg (2¼ lb) shredded vegetable marrow (squash) for the potatoes, using 1 cored green pepper, a little vinegar and 1 bunch chopped dill instead of the bay leaf. When the onion is translucent add the shredded marrow to the pan. Sprinkle with a little vinegar, season with salt and add the chopped dill and cored pepper. Pour in a little boiling water, cover and simmer until tender. Thicken with the sour cream and flour as described above.

Spinach Hungarian Style
Parajfőzelék

INGREDIENTS
1 kg (2¼ lbs) spinach * 1 bread roll * 400 ml (14 oz) milk * 1 garlic clove * salt * freshly ground pepper

Soak the roll in half the quantity of milk. Remove the stems and wash the spinach thoroughly in plenty of water. Bring some water to a boil in a large pan, add salt and the spinach and cook for approximately 5 minutes. Drain

well, then process in an electric blender, adding
the squeezed, soaked roll. Blend the remaining
milk with 2 level tbs flour until smooth. Heat in
a large pan over low heat stirring constantly
until it thickens. Add the spinach and stir well,
adding a little more milk if it is too thick.
Season with salt and freshly ground pepper and
add the crushed garlic. Simmer for a few more
minutes before serving.

Kohlrabi, Carrots or Peas Hungarian Style

*Karalábéfőzelék, sárgarépafőzelék,
zöldborsófőzelék*

INGREDIENTS

1 kg (2¼ lbs) kohlrabi, diced carrots or 1 kg peas *
50 g (2 oz) butter or 2 tbs oil * salt * 1 tsp sugar *
1 tbs flour * 1 bunch parsley * a little milk

Peel the kohlrabi and cut into thin strips
(2–3 cm–1 in long). Put the kohlrabi, carrots or
peas into a pan. Add the butter or oil, the salt
and sugar and a little boiling water. Cover and
simmer until tender. Remove the lid and cook
until the liquid is reduced. Sprinkle with the
flour, add a little milk and stir until the liquid
thickens, for 1–2 minutes. Sprinkle with plenty
of chopped parsley before serving. These
vegetables are often served cooked together, in
which case use a third of the quantity of each
and follow the recipe above.

Kidney Beans, Split Peas or Lentils Hungarian Style

Szemesbabfőzelék, sárgaborsófőzelék, lencsefőzelék

INGREDIENTS

400 g (14 oz) kidney beans, split peas or lentils (all soaked overnight) * 2 tbs oil * 1 small grated onion * 2 level tbs flour * salt * 1–2 bay leaves for lentils * 2 garlic cloves for the beans

Soak the beans, peas or lentils overnight in cold water. Drain, put in a pan and cook in slightly salted, boiling water until tender. If preparing lentils, add bay leaf to the pan. In another pan fry the grated onion in the oil until translucent–if you are cooking beans, add the crushed garlic. Coat the onion with the flour and sauté until light brown. Pour in a little cold water, stir until smooth, and pour over the vegetables. Cook over medium heat, stirring until the liquid thickens. Process the split peas in an electric blender before serving and sprinkle the top with thin slices of onion dipped in flour and deep fried in oil.

Dumplings

Galuska

INGREDIENTS

200 g (7 oz) plain flour * 2 eggs * 2 tbs oil or 50 g (2 oz) butter * salt

Tip the flour into a large bowl and add ¹/₂ tsp salt. Make a well in the center and gradually beat in the eggs and enough cold water to make a stiff dough; put aside for 30 minutes. Bring some water to the boil and add a little salt. Place the galuska dough on a chopping board and using a knife cut off small pieces of the dough and drop them into the boiling water, a few at a time. Stir frequently to prevent the noodles from sticking together or to the bottom of the pan. When they rise to the surface remove with a perforated spoon. Rinse in hot water, drain well and then fry in the hot butter or oil for a few minutes. Serve immediately in a warmed serving dish. Galuska is traditionally served with stews and chicken paprika.

Egg Barley
Tarhonya

Today tarhonya may be bought ready–made in the shops just like any other dry pasta. However, if you wish to prepare it yourself, this is how it is done:

INGREDIENTS
3 eggs * flour * salt * 3 tbs oil (for cooking) * salt * generous pinch of paprika

Beat the eggs thoroughly and add a pinch of salt. Gradually add enough flour to make a fairly stiff dough. Lay on a floured surface and knead until smooth. Shape into a ball, sprinkle with flour, cover and put aside for 30 minutes. Roll out on a floured surface and using fingers dipped in flour shape into small, round pea–size noodles. Spread them out and leave to dry for at least one hour or longer. Heat the oil in a thick saucepan. Add the noodles and fry over high heat until light brown, stirring constantly. Sprinkle with a generous pinch of paprika, pour in enough boiling water to cover and season with salt to taste. Cover and cook over a gentle heat, stirring occasionally until the noodles are soft and all the liquid has been absorbed.

Main Dishes

Potato paprika

Hungarian ratatouille (Lecsó)

Roast carp

Stew with sauerkraut (Székely gulyás)

Stuffed cabbage Kolozsvár style

Budapest steak

Steak Kedvessy style

Sirloin steak Esterházy style

Csáky sirloin

Hungarian stew (Pörkölt)

Wine cellar stew

Veal paprika

Magyaróvár style baked veal

Marchal liver

Fried liver

Brain and kidney

Bakony style pork

Gipsy pork slices

Robber's meat on a skewer

Pork and potato casserole

Chicken paprika (Csirkepaprikás)

Potato Paprika

Serpenyős burgonya (paprikás krumpli)

The potato was not introduced into Hungary until the middle of the 17th century when a group of German Protestant students arrived in Budapest with some examples of this unfamiliar vegetable. They actually got into trouble for doing so. The common belief at that time was that these tubers were poisonous. The hapless students were duly thrown into the Buda dungeon. The Palatine of Hungary himself led the inquiry and learned from German Swabians living on the outskirts of the town that the potato was indeed edible. He therefore ordered that a few of these tubers be cooked there and then. The delicious, mouthwatering aroma that pervaded the hall enticed him to taste them himself. He was so impressed he ordered the immediate release of the students and the propagation of the potato. However, it took another hundred years before the Hungarians really accepted the "German pumpkin" as they called it. By the 19th century the potato became one of the commonest and cheapest vegetables in the country. Potato paprika today is most often served in Hungarian homes rather than restaurants.

INGREDIENTS

1 kg (2¼ lbs) potato * 100 g (4 oz) smoked streaky bacon or 2 tbs oil * 1 medium onion * 300–400 g (13–14 oz) German sausage or frankfurters * 1 tomato * 1 green or yellow pepper * 100 ml (4 oz) sour cream * salt * 1 tbs paprika

---

Dice and fry the bacon in a large pan until cisp, then sauté the finely chopped onion until translucent. Sprinkle with the paprika, add the peeled and diced potatoes, and add a little boiling water. Finally add the quartered tomato and the cored and quartered pepper. Season with salt, cover and simmer, stirring occasionally until the potato is soft. Halfway through the cooking time, add the sliced sausage or frankfurters. Stir in the sour cream, simmer for another minute or two, and serve with pickled vegetables.

Hungarian Ratatouille
Lecsó

As soon as summer arrives and the tomatoes and the special yellow peppers peculiar to Hungary appear in the market, *lecsó* (pronounced lecho) is a frequent and very popular dish, prepared both in Hungarian homes and most restaurants. It is often cooked outside on an open fire. The basic ingredients are onions, tomatoes and peppers but a variety of additional ingredients, such as sliced frankfurters, eggs, spicy sausage or rice, may also be added.

INGREDIENTS
1 kg (2^1/4 lbs) green or yellow peppers * 300 g (11 oz) tomatoes * 1 large onion * 1–3 garlic cloves * 100 g (4 oz) fat, smoked bacon or 2 tbs oil * salt
Additional ingredients to the basic lecsó: 4 eggs, 8 frankfurters or 100 g (4 oz) rice

Dice the bacon and sauté with the finely chopped onion in a large pan until the onion is translucent. Skin the tomatoes and cut them into small wedges, mince the garlic and add both to the pan. When the juice from the tomatoes runs,

add the halved, cored and thinly sliced peppers.
Season with salt, cover and simmer until the
peppers are cooked. If you are adding sausage or
frankfurters, cut it into slices and cook in the
pan for 5 minutes. If you are making *lecsó* with
eggs, remove the lid from the pan and cook until
the liquid has been reduced before adding the
beaten eggs. Stir until the eggs begin to solidify.
For *lecsó* with rice, add the uncooked rice to the
pan after the green peppers so that it can cook in
the liquid. You might have to add a little boiling
water, though.

Roast Carp
Rácponty

Carp is a very popular fish in Hungary. This
particular manner of preparation using green
peppers and tomatoes, came from the Serbs who
settled in Hungary.

INGREDIENTS
1kg 200 g carp (2 lb 11 oz) * 200 g (7 oz) lean smoked
bacon * 1kg (2¼ lbs) potatoes * 300 g (11 oz) green or
yellow peppers * 300 g (11 oz) tomatoes * 1 large onion
*200 ml (7 oz) sour cream * salt * good pinch paprika

Clean the fish and sprinkle the inside with salt.
Make a few cuts across the backbone. Cut the
bacon into thin strips and fit a slice into each
cut. Line an oblong fireproof dish with the
remaining sliced bacon. Peel and slice the
potatoes and lay them in a single layer on top of
the bacon. Season with a little salt and bake in a
hot oven for 30 minutes. Place a layer each of
sliced peppers, tomatoes and onions on the
potatoes. Lay the fish on the bed of vegetables

and return to a hot oven for another 30 minutes.
Stir the paprika into the sour cream and pour
over the top. Bake for another 10 minutes, then
serve.

Stew with Sauerkraut
Székelygulyás

János Székely worked as the manager of the
National Theatre in Budapest in the second half
of the last century. There were often visitors to
the Székely's house and his wife soon became
famous for her excellent cooking. The young
members of the cast, who were often penniless
and always hungry, used to visit the house every
day, knowing that they would get a hot meal.
Mrs. Székely found it difficult to cook enough to
satisfy everyone at her table. However, she was
a very resourceful woman and managed to create
many nourishing and satisfying meals. Székely
"goulash" is such a dish.

INGREDIENTS
500 g (1 lb 2 oz) leg of pork or boned knuckle *
150 g (5 oz) smoked fat bacon or 3 tbs oil * 1 large
onion * 1 kg (2^1/$_4$ lbs) sauerkraut * 200 ml (7 oz) sour
cream * 1 tsp flour * 1 tbs paprika * 1 tomato *
1 green or yellow pepper

Heat the oil or fry the diced bacon. Add the
finely chopped onion and sauté until translucent.
Add the cubed meat and brown over high heat
to seal in the juices. Sprinkle with paprika, add
the skinned and sliced tomato, the cored and
sliced pepper and enough boiling water to cover.
Season with salt, cover and simmer until the
meat is almost tender. Meanwhile, squeeze the

liquid out of the sauerkraut and cook in boiling
water for 10 minutes, then drain. Stir into the
pork stew and continue to simmer until the meat
is done. Finally, remove the lid, increase the
heat and cook to reduce the liquid. Blend the
sour cream with the flour, stir into the pan and
cook until the liquid thickens. This dish is
traditionally served with fresh white bread.

Stuffed Cabbage Kolozsvár Style
Kolozsvári töltött káposzta

This stuffed cabbage recipe is one of the richest
Hungarian dishes and is best served in winter as
a meal on its own. This particular variation is
the most satisfying of all.

Rózsa Déry was an actress before the
establishment of permanent theater companies in
the first half of the 19th century. She worked as
a strolling player performing all over the
country, receiving great acclaim wherever she
went. On the occasion of her performance in the
town of Kolozsvár, a great feast was prepared in
her honour. It was the main dish that impressed
her the most. "This dish is obviously only
prepared when a pig has just been
slaughtered...," she wrote, then went on to
describe how it was made. "A layer of pig skin
was put in the bottom of an enormous pan
followed by sauerkraut, prepared in the same
way as I do it myself. Then layers of black
pudding, bacon and pieces of pork followed.
Then they placed some more sauerkraut on top,
and a larded roast chicken and still more
sauerkraut, sausage, bacon and pork. Water was
then poured in, enough to cover. Then the whole
thing was covered with another layer of pork

skin and cooked.... It was truly delicious but rather expensive." Although this dish has been simplified over the years we feel it is still very good.

INGREDIENTS

1kg ($2^{1}/_{4}$ lbs) sauerkraut * 3 large cabbage leaves * 500 g (1 lb 2 oz) minced pork * 500 g (1 lb 2 oz) leg of pork * 4 pork chops * 250 g (9 oz) spicy sausage * 50 g (2 oz) rice * 1 egg * 100 g (4 oz) lean smoked bacon * 4 tbs oil * 1 tbs flour * 1 large onion * 3–4 garlic cloves * 200 ml (7 oz) sour cream * 1 tbs tomato purée * salt * freshly ground pepper * 1 tsp paprika

---

Place the rice in a pan, add enough boiling water to cover and cook over a gentle heat until it has absorbed all the liquid. When done, mix thoroughly with the minced pork and the egg. Season with salt and pepper. Cut the three cabbage leaves into four and remove the stalks. Place a small mound of the filling in the center of each piece of cabbage leaf. Fold the two ends of each leaf over, then roll it up. Dice and fry the bacon in 1 tbs of oil in a large saucepan. Dice the onion, add to the pan and sauté until translucent. Cut the loin or leg of pork into strips and fry in the pan over a medium heat, then sprinkle with the paprika. Add half the squeezed, shredded sauerkraut in a layer over the pork, then place the stuffed cabbage leaves on top. Sprinkle with the diced garlic and cover it with the remaining sauerkraut. Pour in enough boiling water to cover and carefully stir in the tomato purée. Cover and simmer for 40 minutes. Remove the stuffed cabbage leaves and put aside, while continuing to simmer the sauerkraut for another hour. Make a roux in a large pan with 2 tbs of oil and the flour. Pour in a little

water and stir until smooth, then add the
sauerkraut and cook until the liquid thickens,
stirring all the time. Return the stuffed cabbage
leaves to the pan and simmer very gently for
another 30 minutes, stirring occasionally to stop
the cabbage from sticking. Beat the pork chops a
little with a meat tenderizer. Rub with salt and
freshly ground pepper and fry on both sides in
the remaining 1 tbs oil. Cut the sausage into
four and fry in the same oil. Pile the sauerkraut
and the stuffed cabbage leaves into a serving
dish, then lay the chops and sausage on top.
Pour over the sour cream and serve with fresh
bread.

Budapest Steak
Budapest bélszin

INGREDIENTS
4 thick steaks (entrecôte or fillet appr. 150 g–5 oz each) *
30 g (1¹/₂ oz) butter * 2 tbs oil * 50 g (2 oz) smoked fat
bacon * 1 onion * 4 peppers * 1 tomato * 150 g (5 oz)
mushrooms * 100 g (4 oz) tinned or cooked frozen peas *
100 g (4 oz) goose liver * 1 beef fouillon cube * salt *
1 tsp paprika * freshly ground pepper *mustard *
150 g (6 oz) steamed rice

Peel and dice the onion and sauté in the oil until
translucent. Sprinkle with the paprika and add
one of the cored and sliced peppers and the
skinned and chopped tomato. Stir in the bouillon
cube, add a little water and simmer for 30
minutes. Process in an electric blender. Fry the
diced bacon in a large pan until crisp, then add
the chopped mushrooms, two of the peppers
cored and thinly sliced, and the cubed goose
liver. Simmer for a few minutes. Pour in the

sauce and simmer until the pepper is tender, then stir in the drained peas. Remove from heat and keep warm. Rub the steak with freshly ground pepper and a small amount of mustard, then fry in the butter. Spread the cooked, heated rice in a warmed serving dish, arrange the steak on top and pour the sauce over it. Garnish with the remaining pepper, cored and finely sliced.

Steak Kedvessy Style
Kedvessy bélszin

Nándor Kedvessy was one of the great chefs in Hungary before the turn of the century. He was greatly influenced by the sophisticated dishes from France and spent some time in Paris learning the secrets of French cooking. He returned to Hungary in 1890 and worked in several of the most elegant restaurants in Budapest. His original style revolutionized Hungarian cuisine. He created numerous dishes of which this is one of his best.

INGREDIENTS
4 thick steaks (entrecôte or fillet) approx. 150 g (5 oz) each * 4 slices goose liver * 150 g (9 oz) mushrooms * 4 white dinner rolls or 4 slices of bread * 100 g (4 oz) butter * salt * freshly ground pepper * mustard
For the sauce: 1 tbs oil * 1 small onion * 1 tomato * 1 green or yellow pepper * 200 ml (7 oz) single cream * 1 level tbs flour * salt * 1 tbs paprika * 1 bunch dill

To prepare the sauce, dice the onion and sauté in the oil until translucent. Sprinkle with the paprika and add the skinned, chopped tomato and the cored, chopped pepper. Season with salt, pour in a little water, cover and simmer until the pepper and tomato have disintegrated. Add a little more boiling water if the liquid evaporates. Finally blend the cream and flour until smooth, and strain into the pan. Add the chopped dill and cook over a moderate heat for 3 minutes, stirring until the liquid thickens. Keep warm. While the sauce cooks, wash and dice the mushrooms and cook gently in 25 g (1 oz) of the butter.

Season with salt and freshly ground pepper and cook until all the liquid has evaporated. Put aside and keep warm. Slice the rolls or the bread the same size as the steak, then fry in 25 g (1 oz) of the butter on both sides. Arrange on a warmed serving dish and cover with the cooked mushrooms. Rub the steak with the pepper and mustard and fry on both sides in the remaining butter, then place on the bread. Sprinkle with salt and keep warm. Finally fry the slices of goose liver and put on top of the steak. Cover with the hot sauce and serve immediately. French fries and peas go well with the steak.

Sirloin Steak Esterházy Style
Esterházy rostélyos

In past centuries the aristocratic Esterházy family played a prominent part in Hungarian history. Successive generations have produced scientists, priests and soldiers, whose good deeds have brought honour and prestige to the family and country. They owned countless estates and lived in greater grandeur than the king himself. They also became the patrons of many great composers, including Beethoven and Haydn. There were also prominent political figures among the family, such as Prince Pál Antal

Esterházy, who once served as the Minister of the Interior.

However, he is not remembered for his role as a politician, but rather as someone who did his best to squander priceless riches and vast sums of money. He became the black sheep of the family. He was a extravagant gourmet and did not care how much time or money was spent on good food and drink. It was in his honour that a chef created this special dish.

INGREDIENTS

1 kg–2$\frac{1}{4}$ lbs sirloin steak * 1 large onion * 2 garlic cloves * 2 carrots * 1 parsnip * 2 tbs oil * 2–3 tbs flour * 200 ml (7 oz) sour cream * 300 ml ($\frac{1}{2}$ pt) dry white wine * salt * 1 tbs paprika * good pinch freshly ground pepper * 1 bay leaf * 1 tsp capers * grated rind and juice of $\frac{1}{4}$ lemon

---

Peel and dice the onion and sauté in a large pan in the oil until translucent. Cut the meat into four large slices. Beat with a tenderizer, dip in flour and add to the pan. Fry over a medium heat on both sides. Clean and slice the carrot and parsnip and add to the pan. Sprinkle with paprika, add the wine and season with salt, pepper and the grated lemon rind. Cover and simmer until tender, adding a little boiling water if the liquid evaporates. Stir the pan occasionally to stop the sauce from sticking. When the meat is tender, arrange in a warmed serving dish and keep hot. Stir the sour cream and sauces together, add a little lemon juice and process in a blender. Stir in the capers and pour the sauce over the meat. Serve with steamed rice.

Csáky Sirloin

Csáky rostélyos

Csáky sirloin seems to have all the ingredients of a really old traditional Hungarian dish. However, it was not created until the 20th century by a renowned cook, Sándor Csáky, who worked in one of Hungary's most prestigious hotels. He combined *lecsó* (Hungarian ratatouille) with sirloin steak.

INGREDIENTS

4 slices (1 kg–2$\frac{1}{4}$ lbs) sirloin steak * 2 onions * 1 garlic clove * 300 g (11 oz) green or yellow peppers * 150 g (5 oz) tomato * 3 eggs * 100 g (4 oz) lean streaky smoked bacon * 2 tbs oil * 200 ml (7 oz) sour cream * salt * 2 generous pinch paprika * pinch ground caraway

---

Dice the bacon and fry in a large saucepan. Peel and finely chop one of the onions and add to the pan. Cover and sauté until the onion is translucent. Sprinkle with a generous pinch of paprika and add the skinned and chopped tomato, the cored and sliced pepper, and the crushed garlic. Cover and simmer until the pepper is tender. Remove the lid and cook over high heat to reduce the liquid, then add the beaten egg. Stir over moderate heat until the eggs begin to solidify. Beat the meat slices until thin, heap the *lecsó* in the middle of each slice. Fold over two ends of the meat, then roll up and secure with meat skewers or satay sticks. Heat the oil in a large pan, add the second onion, peeled and chopped, and sauté until translucent. Add the meat rolls and fry over medium heat on both sides. Add a pinch of paprika and a little

boiling water. Season with salt and the ground
caraway seeds. Cover and simmer until tender,
stirring occasionally. Remove the lid and cook
to reduce the liquid, then carefully lift out the
meat rolls, remove the skewers and arrange
them, cut diagonally in half, on a warmed
serving dish. Add the sour cream to the juice in
the pan and heat through. Pour over the meat
and serve with boiled potatoes.

Hungarian Stew
Pörkölt

Traditional Hungarian stew can be prepared with
any type of meat (beef, pork, poultry, lamb or
even tripe).

INGREDIENTS
1 kg (2¹/₄ lbs) meat * 2 tbs oil * 1 large onion *
2–3 garlic cloves * 1 yellow or green pepper *
1 tomato * salt * 1 tbs paprika * ¹/₂ tsp freshly ground
pepper * ¹/₂ tsp ground caraway seed

Peel and dice the onion. Heat the oil in a large
pan and sauté the onion until translucent. Cut
the meat into cubes (2–3 cm–1–1¹/₂ in) and add
to the pan. Fry over high heat, stirring all the
time to seal in the juices. Sprinkle with the
paprika and pour in just enough boiling water to
cover. Add the crushed garlic, the freshly ground
pepper and caraway seed, the cored and sliced
pepper and the skinned tomato. Season with salt,
cover and simmer until the meat is tender. If the
liquid evaporates during cooking, add boiling
water as needed. Remove the lid and reduce the
liquid until the sauce is thick. Serve piping hot

with boiled potatoes, Hungarian noodles
(galuska) (see p. 37) and cucumber salad
(see p. 31).

Wine Cellar Stew
Pincepörkölt

It will be difficult to find this stew on any
restaurant menu but if you plan on going to a
wine tasting expedition you will probably find it
being prepared in the wine cellar, or in a wine
bar. Originally this dish used to be prepared at
grape harvest time over an open fire outside the
many wine cellars of Hungary. It was usually
made with beef or lamb and was sprinkled with
wine from the previous year's vintage.
Nowadays it is also prepared in the home.

INGREDIENTS

1 kg ($2^{1}/_{4}$ lbs) rump or lean stewing steak * 2 tbs
oil * 1 onion * 2 garlic cloves * 1 litre ($1^{3}/_{4}$ pt) red
wine * salt * freshly ground pepper * 1 tsp paprika *
generous pinch thyme * generous pinch basil

Peel and chop the onion and sauté it in the oil in
a large pan until translucent, sprinkle with the
paprika and add the meat cut into 2 cm (1 in)
cubes. Stir the meat over medium heat for a few
minutes, then pour in enough wine to cover.
Add the salt, pepper and herbs. Cover and cook
over gentle heat, adding more wine as the liquid
evaporates. By the time the meat is tender, it
should have absorbed all the wine, leaving a
thick, delicious sauce at the bottom of the pan.
This *pörkölt* is especially tasty when eaten with
fresh bread and a glass of good red wine.

Veal Paprika
Borjúpaprikás

No visitor should leave Hungary without tasting
veal paprika. It contains all the traditional
ingredients that are characeristic of Hungarian
cooking–succulent veal, paprika and cream. Up
until the first half of this century it was quite
common on Sundays for families, particularly
the men, to treat themselves to quite a
substantial snack between breakfast and lunch.
Half a portion of veal paprika with a pint of
beer was one of their favorites.

INGREDIENTS
800 g (1³/₄ lb) veal * 2 tbs oil * 1 medium onion *
1 green pepper * 1 tomato * 200 ml (7 oz) single cream *
1 heaped tsp flour * salt * 1 tbs sweet paprika.
For the garnish: 1 tbs sour cream * 1 small green pepper

Peel and finely chop or grate the onion and
sauté in the oil in a large pan until translucent.
Sprinkle with the red paprika and add the cored,
sliced pepper and the skinned, chopped tomato.
Add a little boiling water, cover and simmer,
stirring occasionally for 15 minutes. Cut the veal
into approximately 2 cm (1 in) cubes and add to
the pan, seasoning with a little salt. Cover and
cook gently until tender, adding a little more
boiling water if the liquid evaporates. Finally
blend the cream and flour together until smooth
and pour over the meat. Cook for two or three
more minutes so that the sauce thickens. Serve
in a warmed dish topped with the sour cream
and thin rings of green pepper. *Galuska*
(Hungarian pasta, see p. 37) is usually served
with it.

Magyaróvár Style Baked Veal Slices
Magyaróvári borjúszelet (Óvári szelet)

At the world exhibition in Brussels in 1958 the Hungarian restaurant attracted many visitors. János Rákóczi, a first class chef, created a special dish for the occasion and called it "Magyaróvári" because he added a Hungarian cheese called "óvari". It has since become a favorite dish prepared in restaurants and in the home. Today it is also prepared with chicken, turkey breast or pork.

INGREDIENTS
4 large veal escalopes (approx. 600 g–1¹/₂ lbs) *
200 g (7 oz) mushrooms * 4 large ham slices *
4 large cheese (cheddar) slices * 80 g (3 oz) butter * salt
*freshly ground pepper

Beat the veal until thin with a tenderizer, sprinkle with salt and leave in the refrigerator for 30 minutes. In the meantime dice the mushrooms and sauté in a pan with 50 g (2 oz) of the butter. Season to taste with salt and pepper and simmer until the liquid has evaporated. Fry the veal on both sides over high heat in the remaining butter, then arrange them in a single layer in a fireproof dish. Add the cooked mushrooms to the dish and lay a slice of ham and a slice of cheese on each piece of veal. Put the dish in a hot oven until the cheese melts. Serve with mashed potatoes or steamed rice garnished with chopped parsley, and a green salad.

Marchal Liver
Marchal máj

József Marchal began his catering career in France in the 1850's. As a talented young cook, he became a chef to Napoleon III. From there he travelled to Russia and worked in the Tzar's kitchen. He took part in the Crimean war before returning to Hungary where he became the manager of a restaurant frequented by the Hungarian aristocracy. He was the first who tried to popularize French cooking in Hungary. In 1867 he was awarded the honor of planning and preparing the dinner for the crowning ceremony of Francis Joseph. He later bought the Queen of England Hotel in Pest where the wealthiest visitors from abroad stayed and where he passed on his vast knowledge to many young cooks.

INGREDIENTS

800 g (1³/4 lbs) veal or calf's liver * 250 g (9 oz) lean smoked bacon with the rind attached * 2 tbs flour * salt *freshly ground pepper

Cut the liver and bacon into eight slices. Slash the bacon rind in a few places and fry over high heat until crisp. Remove from the pan and keep warm. Beat the liver lightly with a meat tenderizer, dip in the flour and fry in bacon fat on both sides. Lay on a serving dish, place a piece of bacon on the top of each slice of liver and sprinkle with a little of the bacon fat. Serve with potato purée and pickles.

Fried Liver
Pirított máj

INGREDIENTS
**750 g (1 lb 7 oz) veal or calf's liver * 1 large onion *
2 tbs oil * salt * 1 tbs sweet paprika * pinch of ground
pepper**

Wash and dry the liver; cut it into narrow strips.
Peel and grate the onion, sauté in the oil until
translucent, and sprinkle with red paprika. Add
the liver and fry over high heat for a couple of
minutes. Season with the pepper, stir in 2 tbs
boiling water and remove from heat. Only add
salt when the liver is cooked, otherwise it will
turn hard.

Serve with boiled potatoes and pickles.

Brain and Kidney
Vese-velő

INGREDIENTS
**600 g (1 lb 6 oz) pork kidney * 400 g (14 oz) calf brains *
2 tbs oil * 1 small onion * salt * pinch paprika *
1 tsp marjoram**

Cut the kidneys in half lengthways, remove the
core and the outer membrane, and cut into thin
strips. Peel and finely chop the onion. Heat the
oil in a pan and sauté the onions until translucent. Sprinkle with the paprika. Add the
kidneys, sprinkle with the marjoram and fry over
high heat for 3–4 minutes, stirring constantly.
Finally remove the membrane from the brain
and cut into small pieces. Add to the pan and

cook, stirring frequently, until the brain begins to solidify. Season with salt to taste just before serving. Serve with boiled potatoes.

Bakony Style Pork
Bakonyi sertésborda

INGREDIENTS

8 slices (800 g–1³/₄ lb) boned pork chop * 4 slices lean salted bacon * 1 medium onion * 500 g (1 lb 2 oz) mushrooms * freshly ground pepper * paprika * garlic powder * 200 ml (7 oz) sour cream

Beat the meat slices with a meat tenderizer and rub with pepper, paprika and garlic powder. Cut the bacon into cubes. Fry until crisp, then remove from the pan and put aside. Fry the meat in the bacon fat until done, then arrange in a warmed serving dish with the slices overlapping slightly and keep hot. Return the bacon pieces to the pan, sauté the finely chopped onions until translucent and add the sliced mushrooms. Season to taste with paprika, salt and pepper. Simmer until the mushrooms are cooked. Stir in the sour cream, simmer for a few more minutes, then pour over the meat. Serve with *galuska* (Hungarian pasta, see p. 37)

Gipsy Pork Slices
Cigánypecsenye

This dish is often cooked outside on an open fire. Before frying the meat is rubbed with salt, garlic, pepper, paprika and mustard. Here is a very easy variation.

4 large slices (800 g–1 lb 13 oz) pork * 1 tsp oil *
400 ml (14 oz) sour cream * salt * 2 tbs mustard

Beat the pork slices with a meat tenderizer and
sprinkle with salt. Rub a baking dish with the
oil. Blend the sour cream and mustard in a bowl
until smooth then dip the pork slices into the
bowl, one at a time. Place in the baking tray,
pour the remaining sour cream and mustard on
top and cook in a hot oven until the meat has
absorbed almost all the sour cream. Serve with
potato purée and pickled vegetables.

Robber's Meat on a Skewer
Rablópecsenye (Rablóhús)

INGREDIENTS
500 g (1 lb 2 oz) de-boned pork chops * 300 g (11 oz)
large mushrooms * 300 g (11 oz) small onions *
150 g (5 oz) smoked bacon * 1–2 green peppers * 1 tbs oil
* salt * freshly ground pepper

Cut the meat into 5 cm (2^1/$_2$ in) squares. Slice
the bacon thinly into squares roughly the same
size as the pork. Peel the onions and wash the
mushrooms, leaving them whole.

Core the pepper and cut into similar pieces.
Alternating the ingredients, thread them onto
meat skewers or wooden satay sticks. Sprinkle
with salt and pepper and brush with the oil. Lay
the skewers in a baking pan so that they are
balanced on the sides of the pan. Bake in a hot
oven until cooked, serve with mustard and
pickled vegetables, especially cabbage.

Pork and Potato Casserole
Brassói aprópecsenye

This is a very popular dish and has numerous
variations.

INGREDIENTS
600 g (1 lb 6 oz) lean de-boned chops or leg of pork *
400 g (14 oz) potatoes * oil for deep frying * 1 meat stock
cube * salt * freshly ground pepper * 1 tsp paprika *
1/2 tsp marjoram

Slice the pork then cut into narrow strips. Fry
over high heat in 2 tbs oil for 3 minutes stirring
constantly, sprinkle with pepper and marjoram.
Crumble the stock cube on top of the meat,
cover and simmer until tender, adding a little
boiling water if the liquid evaporates.
Meanwhile peel and thin-slice the potatoes. Fry
in plenty of oil until golden brown. Place on
paper towel. When the meat is tender add the
chips, season with the paprika and simmer for a
few minutes until the potato chips soften. Serve
with salad.

Chicken Paprika
Csirkepaprikás

INGREDIENTS
Approx. 1.2 kg (1 lb 7 oz) chicken * 2 tbs oil * 1 large
onion * 2 garlic cloves * 1 green pepper * 1 tomato *
100 fl (4 oz) sour cream * 100 fl (4 oz) single cream *
1 level tbs flour * salt * 1 tbs sweet paprika *
For serving: * 1–2 tbs additional sour cream *
1 small pepper

Cut up the chicken into 14 pieces. (The giblets and liver can also be added.) This dish is actually prepared exactly the same way as veal paprika (see p. 54), except that a mixture of cream and sour cream is used. Serve with *galuska* (Hungarian pasta, see p. 37)

Savoury Pasta and other Dishes

Cabbage squares

Pasta and cottage cheese

Crackling scones

Hungarian fried bread (Lángos)

These dishes are traditionally served as a "dessert" in Hungary for those who prefer them to sweet desserts.

Cabbage Squares
Káposztás kocka

INGREDIENTS

200 g (7 oz) large square pasta * 1 kg (2¼ lb) white cabbage * 3 tbs oil * 1 tbs sugar * salt * freshly ground pepper

---

Shred the cabbage finely, removing the core. Sprinkle with a little salt and put aside for one hour. Heat the oil in a large pan, add the sugar and cabbage; fry until golden brown, stirring frequently. Cook the pasta squares in plenty of boiling salted water. Rinse in hot water, drain thoroughly. Stir the cabbage and pasta in the pan. Heat together for a few minutes, then serve sprinkled generously with pepper.

Pasta and Cottage Cheese
Túrós csusza

INGREDIENTS

200 g (7 oz) pasta squares (if you are making your own pasta use 200 g–7 oz plain flour and 2 eggs) * 200 g (7 oz) cottage cheese * 150 g (5 oz) lean smoked bacon * 200 ml (7 oz) sour cream * salt

---

Cook the pasta in plenty of boiling salted water. (If you are preparing your own, put the flour into a bowl with a pinch of salt, make a well in the middle, and gradually blend in the beaten eggs and enough cold water to make a pliable dough. Cover with a cloth and set aside for 30 minutes. Then roll out thin and cut in squares (roughly 5 cm–2½ in) and cook. Meanwhile, dice the bacon and fry until crisp. Remove the bacon pieces and put aside. When the pasta is done, rinse in hot water and drain thoroughly. Turn the pasta in the hot bacon fat until it has heated through. Place in a warmed serving dish, sprinkle with sour cream and top with the bacon pieces. Serve immediately, or re-heat.

Crackling Scones
Töpörtyűs pogácsa

Four-hundred years ago the Turks occupied Hungary and stayed for 150 years. Though they often bought along their own families, they also married Hungarian girls sometimes. They also introduced their own religion, culture and eating habits. There are still many dishes of Turkish origin today. The most popular is a kind of savoury scone. It has obviously changed over the years and has many variations. It is sometimes made from flaky or puff pastry or with yeast. Cheese, ham or cabbage can also be added. The most popular, however, is the scone with crackling.

INGREDIENTS
400 g (14 oz) plain flour * 30 g (1½ oz) yeast * milk * 1 tsp sugar * 2 egg yolks * 150 pork (5 oz) crackling * 50 g (2 oz) pork fat * 1 tsp salt * 1 egg or the 2 beaten egg whites for brushing

Heat 3 tbs milk with the sugar until lukewarm. Add the crumbled yeast and leave in a warm place until the yeast has dissolved. Put the flour and salt in a bowl, add the yeast, the egg yolks and enough lukewarm milk to make a fairly stiff dough. Finally knead in the melted pork fat. Shape into a ball, cover with a cloth and leave in a warm place for one hour. Then roll out to finger thickness and sprinkle evenly with half the grated crackling. Roll up tightly, fold each end over, cover and leave in a warm place for 20 minutes. Roll out again, sprinkle with the remaining crackling. Repeat the procedure and leave for another 20 minutes. Finally roll out to the thickness of two fingers and cut into rounds with a 5 cm (2^1/$_2$ in) fluted pastry cutter. Place on a greased baking tray and score the top of the scones in a lattice pattern with a knife. Brush with the beaten egg or egg whites and bake in a hot oven for 8 minutes, then reduce the oven to a low heat and bake until golden brown. These scones are equally good served hot, warm or cold and go well with a glass of beer.

Hungarian Fried Bread
Lángos

Bread has been baked since ancient times. Traditional Hungarian bread is very tasty because the wheat grown in the Carpathian basin is especially good. When every family baked their own bread, a little piece of dough was always left over to make *lángos*. They were rolled into the size of a hand and about finger thickness and then baked separately. Today they are not baked in the oven but deep fried in oil; usually the dough also contains potatoes as well. Lángos is extremely popular in Hungary, rather like fish and chips in England. They are eaten just sprinkled with salt, brushed with garlic and paprika or sour cream, and sprinkled with grated cheese.

INGREDIENTS

500 g (1 lb 2 oz) flour * 1 egg (optional) * 30 g (1$^{1}/_{2}$ oz) yeast * milk * 1 tsp sugar * 200 g (7 oz) potatoes * 2 tbs oil * 1 level tsp salt * oil for deep frying

Cook the potatoes in boiling water, peel and mash. Meanwhile, soften the yeast in 3 tbs lukewarm milk and the sugar; set aside. Put the mashed potatoes and flour into a bowl, add the yeast mixture, the egg and enough lukewarm milk to make a fairly stiff dough. Knead in the salt and the oil, shape into a ball, cover and leave in a warm place until double in size. Then roll out to finger thickness, cut into rounds (approx. 20 cm–7 in in diameter) and fry in plenty of hot oil until golden brown.

Desserts

Cottage cheese dumplings

Plum dumplings

Gundel pancake

Hot noodle cake *(Vargabéles)*

Hungarian strudel *(Rétes)*

Rákóczi cottage cheese squares

Spong cake with vanilla and chocolate sauce
(Somlói galuska)

Gerbeaud slice

Rigó Jancsi *(Hungarian eclairs)*

Indian's Head *(Indiáner)*

Dobos torte

Cottage Cheese Dumplings
Túrógombóc

INGREDIENTS

500 g (1 lb 2 oz) low fat cottage cheese * 3 tbs semolina * 3 eggs * 50 g (2 oz) butter * 1 tbs oil * 4–5 tbs bread-crumbs * salt * vanilla powdered sugar

Mash the cottage cheese, blend with the semolina, eggs and a pinch of salt. Knead well and set aside for about 4 hours. Dipping your fingers in cold water, shape the mixture into small round dumplings (approx. 5 cm–2$^1/_2$ in) and cook in plenty of salted boiling water for 5 minutes (To test if they are done, cut one in half and see if the center is cooked.) While the dumplings are cooking, sauté the breadcrumbs in a mixture of the oil and butter. Remove the dumplings with a perforated spoon and drain thoroughly. Place them into the pan of breadcrumbs and shake the pan gently to coat the dumplings all over. Serve at once dusted with vanilla powdered sugar.

Plum Dumplings
Szilvásgombóc

INGREDIENTS

600 g (1 lb 6 oz) mashed potatoes * 200 g (7 oz) plain flour * 1 kg (2$^1/_4$ lbs) plums * 1 egg * 1 tbs oil * sugar * 4 tbs breadcrumbs * cinnamon * powdered sugar * 50 g (2 oz) butter or 2–3 tbs oil

Put the mashed potato into a bowl, add a pinch of salt and mix with beaten egg and enough flour to make a soft pliable dough. Work in the

oil. Put on a floured surface and roll out thin.
Cut into squares big enough to cover a plum.
Wash and pit the plums and put a pinch of sugar
and cinnamon inside each one. Place a plum in
the center of each square and pull the corners
together. Roll into balls using floured hands.
Bring a large pan of water to the boil. Add a
little salt and gently drop in the dumplings. Turn
them over occasionally with a wooden spoon to
prevent them from sticking. When the dumplings
come to the surface, cook for an additional 4
minutes. Remove with a perforated spoon and
drain thoroughly. While the dumplings are
cooking, sauté the breadcrumbs in the butter or
oil. Place the dumplings in the pan and, shaking
gently, coat them with the breadcrumbs. Serve
with a mixture of powdered sugar and
cinnamon.

Gundel Pancake
Gundel palacsinta

The Gundel Restaurant is as integral a part of
Budapest as are the Houses of Parliament or the
Chain Bridge. Károly Gundel, the youngest
member of the well known dynasty of chefs,
bought Wampetics Restaurant in 1910 and also
rented the restaurants at the Gellért Hotel and
the Royal. However, the Gundel Restaurant
remained nearest to his heart, and he worked
there with his wife and children. It was here that
he trained a future generation of cooks. Chefs
mastered not only his culinary art but also his
philosophy of life. Károly Gundel also wrote
several excellent cook books, which included
many of his own creations. One of the most
popular is Gundel pancake.

INGREDIENTS

For the pancakes: 200 g (7 oz) plain flour * 2 egg *
200 ml (7 oz) milk * soda water * 2–3 tbs oil * pinch salt
For the filling: 200 g (7 oz) ground walnuts * 150 g (5 oz)
finely granulated sugar * 200 ml (7 oz) single cream *
50 g (2 oz) raisins * a little vanilla sugar * grated rind of
1/4 lemon.
For the sauce: 100 g (4 oz) dark chocolate * 1 egg yolk *
200 ml (7 oz) milk * 100 ml (4 oz) single cream *
1 oz dark rum

Put the flour in a bowl, make a well in the
center. Add the beaten eggs and a little milk and
gradually blend together until smooth. Beat in
the remaining milk and enough soda water to
make a fairly thick batter. Set aside for 30
minutes, then stir in the oil. Fry the pancakes in
the oil on both sides, then lay them on a plate.
To make the filling: heat the cream in a pan,
add the sugar and vanilla sugar and the ground
walnuts. Remove from heat and stir in the
raisins and the grated lemon rind. Place a
spoonful of the mixture in the center of each
pancake then fold in half and fold again.
Arrange slightly overlapping in a fireproof dish.
Break the chocolate into pieces into a pan. Add
the milk and heat slowly until the chocolate has
melted, stirring frequently. Beat the egg yolk
and the cream together and add to the melted
chocolate. Place the pan over steam and heat,
stirring constantly, until the sauce thickens. Then
remove from heat, stir in the rum and pour over
the pancakes. Place in a hot oven or microwave
to heat through. (Although the original Gundel
recipe does not include this, many restaurants
serve it flambéed by pouring a glass of rum over
the pancakes and lighting it.)

Hot Noodle Cake
Vargabéles

According to popular Hungarian belief
vargabáles became a customary dessert served at
weekly and monthly markets where anything
was bought or sold, ranging from pigs, cattle
and fodder to boots and clothes. The cobbler's
(*varga* in Hungarian) stall was a common sight.
According to legend, this sweet with pasta and
cottage cheese was a special favorite among the
shoemakers and that is how it got its name.
However, it is more likely that the dessert was
first introduced in a very popular establishment
known as the Varga Restaurant around the turn
of the century in the town of Kolozsvár.

INGREDIENTS

1 packet of frozen strudel or filo dough.
For the filling: 150 g (5 oz) vermicelli or flat noodle*
5 eggs *300 g (11 oz) cottage cheese * 200 ml (7 oz) sour
cream *2 rolls * milk for soaking the rolls * 100 g (4 oz)
powdered sugar * 1 heaped tsp vanilla sugar * grated rind
of 1 lemon * 100 g (4 oz) seedless raisons * 50 g (2 oz)
butter * salt * 1 egg yolk

Leave the pastry to thaw completely. Meanwhile
cook the vermicelli in salted boiling water, rinse
in hot water and drain thoroughly. Put the rolls
in milk to soak. Separate the five eggs, beat the
egg yolks with the powdered sugar and vanilla
sugar in a large bowl, then add the softened
butter. Mash the cottage cheese and add along
with the sour cream. Blend thoroughly, then stir
in the cooked pasta, the grated lemon rind and
the seedless raisins. Squeeze out the excess milk
from the rolls and add to the mixture. Finally
fold in the stiffly beaten egg whites. Divide the

strudel pastry in half and roll out one piece to line a medium sized baking pan 20 x 40 cm (10 x 20 in). Spread the filling on top, then cover with the rest of the pastry. Brush with the beaten egg yolk and prick with a fork. Bake in a hot oven for 10 minutes, then reduce to moderate until golden brown. Remove from oven and leave in the pan for five minutes; cut into 5 cm (2$^{1}/_{2}$ in) squares. They are best served immediately.

Hungarian Strudel
Rétes

INGREDIENTS

4 sheets of strudel or filo pastry * oil.
For apple strudel: 1 kg (2$^{1}/_{4}$ lbs) apples * 3–4 tbs breadcrumbs * 50–100 g (2–4 oz) castor sugar (depending on the sweetness of the apples) * 50 g (2 oz) seedless raisins * a little cinnamon.
For cherry or sour cherry strudel: 1 kg (2$^{1}/_{4}$ lbs) cherries * 2 tbs breadcrumbs * 50 g (2 oz) ground walnuts * 100 g (4 oz) castor sugar * cinnamon.
For strudel with cottage cheese filling: 300 g (11 oz) cottage cheese * 50 g (2 oz) butter * 3 heaped tbs powdered sugar * 3 eggs * 3 tbs milk * 1 tbs flour * 100 g (4 oz) raisins or seedless raisins (optional) * lemon rind

To prepare the apple strudel, peel and grate the apples and simmer with the sugar uncovered until all the liquid has been absorbed. Flavor with a little cinnamon. Using all four sheets of pastry, place two sheets on top of the other two. Sprinkle breadcrumbs in a strip 5 cm (2$^{1}/_{4}$ in) wide along the longer side of the pastry. Spoon half the apple filling on to the breadcrumbs and add the seedless raisins and roll up the two pieces of pastry. Follow the same procedure with the rest of the pastry. Place the two rolls, sealed edges down, on a greased baking tray not too close together. Brush the top with oil and bake in a hot oven until golden brown. Slice while still hot and serve. *For the cherry strudel:* pit the cherries and spread over the breadcrumbs (see above), sprinkle with the sugar, a little cinnamon and the ground walnuts, and roll up. *For the cottage cheese strudel,* beat the egg yolks with the softened butter and the sugar in a large bowl. Then mash the cottage cheese and add to the bowl, followed by the milk and flour. Beat thoroughly until smooth. Add the seedless raisins and fold in the stiffly beaten egg whites. If desired, also add the grated rind of half a lemon can also be added). Spoon the mixture on to the pastry the same way as for the other strudel, roll up, brush with oil and bake.

Rákóczi Cottage Cheese Squares
Rákóczi túrós

János Rákóczi was one of the greatest Hungarian chefs of this century. He studied in Paris and worked in two of the most famous restaurants in Hungary. He worked for nearly twenty years in the restaurant of the Gellért Hotel in Budapest. He has also written several excellent cook books. This dessert is one of his best creations.

INGREDIENTS

For the pastry: 250 g (9 oz) plain flour * 120 g (4$\frac{1}{2}$ oz) butter * 60 g (2 oz) powdered sugar * 2 egg yolks * 100 ml (4 oz) sour cream * pinch salt * 2 heaped tsp baking powder. *For the filling:* 500 g (1 lb 2 oz) cottage cheese * 3 egg yolks * 2 egg whites * 200 ml (7 oz) sour cream * 2 rolls * 50 g (2 oz) breadcrumbs * grated rind of half a lemon. *For the topping:* 3–4 egg whites * 160 g (5 oz) castor sugar * apricot jam

Place the dry ingredients in a bowl, add the lemon rind. Fold in the butter and add the egg yolks and sour cream to make a soft pastry. Cover with a cloth and put in the refrigerator to rest for at least one hour. Roll the pastry out large enough to line a square or oblong pan, prick with a fork and bake in a hot oven until half cooked and very light golden brown. In the meantime, beat the egg yolks and the sugar, add the mashed cottage cheese, the diced rolls and the sour cream. Beat thoroughly, stir in the seedless raisins and the lemon rind. Finally, gently fold in the stiffly beaten egg whites. Spread over the pastry and return to a moderate oven until the pastry is well baked. Remove from the oven. Beat the three egg whites with the castor sugar until stiff and using a pastry bag with a plain or star shaped nozzle, pipe a trellis pattern on top. Alternatively, the egg white could simply be spread on top. Reduce the temperature and return to the oven for a few minutes until the egg whites turn to a light golden brown. Remove from the oven and put blobs of apricot jam in between the trellises. Set aside to cool in the pan, then cut pastry into squares with a knife dipped in boiling water.

Sponge Cake with Vanilla and Chocolate Sauce

Somlói galuska

This dessert is often thought to be a traditional treat, but it was created only in the 1950s. It is usually eaten as a special treat in a restaurant and not prepared at home because it is fairly time consuming. However, if you decide to make it yourself, the delicious taste will be worth your time and energy.

INGREDIENTS

For the cake: 4 eggs * 4 tbs finely granulated sugar *
4 tbs plain flour * 1 tbs cocoa * 2 pinch bicarbonate of
soda. *For the cream:* 2 egg yolks * 2 tbs finely granulated
sugar * 2 tsp vanilla sugar * 1 tsp flour * 500 ml (18 oz)
milk. *For the filling:* 3–4 tbs raspberry or apricot jam *
100 ml (4 oz) milk *2–3 tbs rum * 50 g (2 oz) seedless
raisins * 50 g (2 oz) walnuts * 50 g (2 oz) glazed fruit.
For the topping: 200 ml (7 oz) whipping cream *
1 tbs powdered sugar * 1 tbs finely granulated sugar *
1 tbs cocoa * 20 g ($^1/_2$ oz) butter.

For the sponge cake cream the egg yolks, the
sugar and bicarbonate of soda until light yellow.
Beat in the vanilla sugar and the flour and fold
in the stiffly beaten egg whites. Divide the
mixture in half and add the cocoa to one half.
Line an oblong pan appr. 20 x 40 cm (10 x 20 in)
with lightly oiled bakery paper and smooth the
cocoa flavored mixture in one half of the pan
and the rest in the other half (it does not matter
if they run into each other). Bake in a hot
pre–heated oven for five minutes, then reduce
the heat to low. Bake until golden brown. Test
by inserting a toothpick in the middle of the
cake; if it comes out clean, the cake is done.
Unmold on a cake rack and remove the paper.
When cool, cut in half lengthwise. Sandwich the
halves with the jam and then cut into cubes.
While the cake is baking, prepare the cream by
beating the egg yolks with the sugar and flour
until smooth, then adding the milk, a little at
a time. Place the bowl over steam and stir
constantly until it thickens. Remove from heat,
stir in the vanilla sugar and set aside to cool.
Arrange layers of the sponge cake followed by
layers of cream in a deep glass bowl or in
individual glass bowls, topping it with a layer of
cake. Also add the chopped walnuts, the glazed
fruit and the seedless raisins in between the

layers. Mix the rum and milk together and sprinkle over the top of the cake. Whip the cream with the powdered sugar and smooth over the top. Finally mix the cocoa and castor sugar together in a small pan until smooth, adding a little water as needed. Bring to the boil and stir until it thickens. Remove from the heat and beat in the butter. Pour over the cream in a thin stream.

Gerbeaud Slice
Gerbeaud szelet

About 110 years ago, Henrik Kugler, the most famous pastry cook in Pest, visited Paris where he met a very talented young Swiss confectioner, Emil Gerbeaud. Later Kugler invited Gerbeaud to Pest and as there was no successor in his family to carry on the profession, he asked Gerbeaud to join him. In 1884 they entered into a partnership and the coffee house took on the name of Gerbeaud. In 1910 it was refurbished in the style of Maria Theresa with chandeliers and marble and bronze decor. It still flourishes today under the same name in the heart of Budapest and should not be missed by anyone visiting the city. The coffee is excellent and the choice of delicious cakes and puddings is quite fantastic. This cake is named after the Swiss confectioner who introduced many French and Austrian delicacies to the people of Hungary.

INGREDIENTS
500 g (1 lb 2 oz) plain flour * 250 g (9 oz) butter or margarine * 4 tbs powdered sugar * 1 tsp vanilla sugar * 1 egg yolk * 100 ml (4 oz) sour cream * 10 g (¹/₂ oz) yeast * 3 tbs milk * 1 tsp bicarbonate of soda. *For the filling:*

apricot jam * 250 g (9 oz) ground walnuts * 250 g (9 oz) powdered sugar * 1 tsp vanilla sugar. *For the chocolate icing:* 200 g (7 oz) cooking chocolate * 80 g (3 oz) butter

---

Heat the milk with 1 tsp sugar until lukewarm and pour into a large bowl. Crumble in the yeast and set aside for a short time. Add the flour, sugar and bicarbonate of soda. Mix in the egg yolk and the sour cream and knead quickly together. Shape into a ball, cover with a cloth and chill for one hour. Divide the dough into three equal portions. Roll out one third to line a medium sized oblong baking pan (approx. 20 x 40 cm–10 x 20 in). Spread generously with apricot jam. Mix the ground walnuts and powdered sugar together and sprinkle half over the jam. Roll out the second third of the dought to cover, spread with jam and the remaining walnuts. Roll out the remaining dough to cover the top. Prick with a fork and bake in a moderate pre-heated oven for about 40 minutes until deep golden brown. Set aside to cool in the pan. *To prepare the chocolate icing:* break the chocolate into small pieces and place in a bowl with the butter and vanilla sugar. Place over steam or in a microwave until the chocolate has melted. Cream together and spread over the cake. When it has hardened, cut the cake into slices.

Rigó Jancsi

(Hungarian Eclairs)

In the Christmas of 1895 Paris buzzed with excitement over the performance of a guest artist, the Hungarian gipsy violinist Jancsi Rigó. Though he was not particularly attractive with a pock marked face, his talent captured the hearts of the women wherever he went. Duke Chimay and his beautiful wife attended a performance and apparently the duchess was so enraptured by the music and his dark sparkling eyes, she abandoned her husband and her children for him. This romantic story has inspired novelists, poets, composers and even a film director. When invited to perform in Pest, Jancsi Rigó asked the confectioner at the hotel where he was staying to create a special cake in honor of the beautiful duchess. Rigó Jancsi became one of the most popular cakes and still is to this day.

INGREDIENTS

6 eggs (separated) * 60 g (2 oz) butter * 100 g (4 oz) granulated sugar * 3 small bars bitter chocolate * 60 g (2 oz) plain flour * 100 g (4 oz) ground walnuts or hazelnuts. *For the cream:* 600 ml (1 pt) whipping cream * 6 tsp sugar * 3 heaped tbs cocoa * 1 tsp gelatin * 200 g (7 oz) chocolate for topping the cake

---

Break the bitter chocolate into pieces and place in a bowl over steam until it melts. Beat the egg yolks, sugar and butter until fluffy, then add the melted chocolate and the flour. Finally, fold in the ground walnuts and the stiffly beaten egg whites. Smooth the mixture into an oblong baking pan (approx. 30 x 40 cm–15 x 20 in) lined with oiled bakery paper and bake in a hot pre-heated oven for 12–15 minutes. Use a toothpick to test if it is dóne. Unmold onto a rack, remove the paper and set aside to cool.

Slice in half and spread one piece with the chocolate cream. When the cream has hardened a little, cut the cake into 4 cm (2 in) squares. Beat the cream with the cocoa and sugar until smooth. Pour into a pan and bring to the boil stirring constantly. Remove from heat and set aside to cool. Meanwhile dissolve the gelatin in a little water.

Whisk the cream until stiff, then stir in the gelatin vigorously. Spread thickly over the other half of the cake and place the chocolate glazed squares on top. Dip a knife into hot water and cut right through along the edges.

Indian's Head
Indiáner

In the year 1834 a guest artist of Indian origin was invited to perform at Vienna's most famous theater. The Viennese thronged to watch this exotic spectacle. The manager of the theater, the Hungarian Count Ferdinand Pálffy, organized a dinner in honor of the Indian artist and the chef created a dessert especially for the occasion, calling it "Indiáner". In a few weeks it spread in popularity and soon decorated the windows and shelves of all the good coffee houses of Vienna, Pest and other cities. It is still a favourite today.

INGREDIENTS
6 eggs (separated) * 100 g (4 pz) powdered sugar *
140 g (5 pz) flour * 2 pinch bicarbonate of soda.
For the filling: 400 ml (14 oz) whipping cream *
2 tbs powdered sugar * 200 g (7 oz) chocolate cake
covering * 2 patty tins

Beat the egg yolks with half the sugar and the bicarbonate of soda until pale yellow. Whisk the egg whites with the rest of the sugar until stiff, then fold into the mixture. Finally sift in the flour. Grease the patty tins well and fill half-way with the cake mixture. Place in a hot oven for

5 minutes, then reduce to moderate heat for another 5–8 minutes. Test if they are done with a toothpick. Unmold onto a rack to cool, then cut in half horizontally. Remove a little of the center from each half. Cover the top halves of each cake with the chocolate glaze. Whip the cream until very stiff, then beat in the powdered sugar. Fill the hollowed out bottom halves of the cakes with the cream just before serving and place the chocolate glazed halves on top.

Dobos Torte
Dobos torta

József Dobos opened a large general store in the winter of 1878 in a busy street in Pest. He was from a line of famous cooks. His great grand-father had worked in the kitchens of Prince Rákóczi's castle. Dobos stocked his store with a wide selection of food and drink. He imported Parma ham from Italy, cheese and champagne from Germany and France, and always had a variety of Hungarian wines. He also made his own cold dishes and cakes and was always experimenting and surprising his customers with new inventions. This was how his most famous cake came into being, consisting of five layers of sponge cake sandwiched with chocolate cream with a crisp caramel topping. A hundred years later "dobos torte" is still a favorite in every pastry shop in Budapest and Vienna.

INGREDIENTS
6 eggs * 100 g (4 oz) powdered sugar 100 g (4 oz) plain flour * 350 g (³/4 lb) butter. *For the filling:* 4 eggs (separated) * 200 g (7 oz) powdered sugar * 20 g (¹/2 oz) vanilla sugar * 235 g (¹/2 lb) butter * 350 g (³/4 lb) cocoa butter (or butter if you cannot get

cocoa butter) * 350 g ($^3/_4$ lb) g cocoa powder *
200 g (7 oz) cooking chocolate.
For the caramel topping: 200 g (7 oz) powdered sugar

Beat the egg yolks with half the sugar until pale
yellow, then beat in the sifted flour and the
softened butter. Whisk the egg whites with the
remaining sugar until stiff and fold into the
mixture. Grease and flour six equally sized
round cake pans and divide the mixture between
them. Bake in a hot oven for 3–4 minutes until
light golden brown. *For the cream:* beat the
whole eggs with the powdered sugar then place
over steam and heat, stirring constantly, until it
thickens. Remove from the heat and continue
beating until the mixture cools down. Beat the
butter in another bowl until soft, add the vanilla
sugar and the cocoa. Stir in the melted cocoa
butter and chocolate, and combine with the egg
mixture. Beat thoroughly, then spread on five of
the sponge layers. Lay the sixth layer on top,
pressing it down gently. Melt the sugar in a pan
and heat until it turns into golden brown runny
caramel. Pour onto a buttered plate the same
size as the cake and spread evenly with a
buttered knife. Before it hardens, cut into slices
using a knife dipped in cold water, then place on
the top layer. Some prefer to spread the cake
with a thin layer of apricot jam before placing
the caramel on top.

Kner Printing House
Gyomaendrőd